# Clarence Thomas

## Supreme Court Justice

# Clarence Thomas

## Supreme Court Justice

Warren J. Halliburton

ENSLOW PUBLISHERS, INC.

Bloy St. and Ramsey Ave.      P.O. Box 38
Box 777                      Aldershot
Hillside, N.J. 07205      Hants GU12 6BP
U.S.A.                          U.K.

*Our thanks to Mrs. Leola Williams, mother of Clarence Thomas, for allowing us to use several photographs of her son to illustrate this book.*

Copyright © 1993 by Warren J. Halliburton

**Library of Congress Cataloging-in-Publication Data**

Halliburton, Warren J.
    Clarence Thomas, Supreme Court justice / Warren J. Halliburton.
       p. cm. — (People to know)
    Includes index.
    Summary: Describes the life of the newest justice of the Supreme Court from his childhood in Georgia, through the years he spent as chairman of the EEOC, to the present.
    ISBN 0-89490-414-0
    1. Thomas, Clarence, 1948—Juvenile literature. 2. Judges—United States—Biography—Juvenile literature. 3. United States. Supreme Court—Biography—Juvenile literature. [1. Thomas, Clarence, 1948– . 2. Judges. 3. United States. Supreme Court—Biography. 4. Afro-Americans—Biography.] I. Title. II. Series.
KF8745.T48H35 1993
347.73'2634—dc20
[B]
[347.3073534]
[B]                                                     92-30951
                                           CIP
                                           AC

Printed in the United States of America

10 9 8 7 6 5 4 3 2 1

**Illustration Credits:**
AP/Wide World Photos, pp. 40, 79, 82, 89, 94; Bettmann Archive, p. 21; Collection of the Supreme Court of the United States, p. 86; Courtesy of Leola Williams, pp. 35, 38, 60, 96; Library of Congress, pp. 49, 87; Reuters/Bettmann, pp. 6, 9, 75, 77, 80; Saturday Evening Post, p. 28; Shell Oil Company, p. 25; UPI/Bettmann , p. 92.

**Cover Illustration:**
© National Geographical Society, Courtesy Supreme Court Historical Society.

# Contents

Clarence Thomas

# Introduction

On July 1, 1991 President George Bush called a press conference. It was held at his summer home in Kennebunkport, Maine. Standing at the President's side was a short, well-dressed, dark-skinned man. The man's manner and expression added to the drama and dignity of the occasion. The President said:

> I am very pleased to announce that I will nominate Judge Clarence Thomas to serve as Associate Justice of the United States Supreme Court.
> Clarence Thomas was my first appointee to the U.S. Court of Appeals for the District of Columbia, where he served for over a year. And I believe he'll be a great justice. He's the best person for this position.

Then the President presented Thomas's professional background. He included the candidate's schooling and personal qualifications for the position. Finally, he introduced Thomas and asked him to say a few words.

Thomas thanked the President and expressed how "honored and humbled" he was by the nomination. He remarked further:

> Only in America could this have been possible. I look forward to the confirmation process and an opportunity to be of service once again to my country, and to be an example to those who are where I was and to show them that, indeed, there is hope.

Thomas was referring to himself as an African American. He was recognizing the fact that he had been born into poverty. And he spoke of what that meant. He said that he was of a people who had suffered more than their share of prejudice and discrimination. He declared himself a living example of the American dream. It was possible, he said, for any and everybody of a mind to realize this dream.

President Bush then indicated that they were ready for questions from the press. The reporters' queries came fast and furious. The one that was most often asked concerned Thomas's eight years as head of the Equal Employment Opportunity Commission (EEOC). This government agency is responsible for challenging discrimination in the workplace. Unlawful acts against people because of their race, sex, color, national origin, and religion are investigated by the EEOC.

Thomas's enforcement of the EEOC laws introduced an exception to the agency's policy. He accepted the complaints of individuals. But he rejected those filed by groups. Cases filed by groups are called class-action suits. Thomas's change in policy drew wide criticism. Civil rights leaders personally attacked Thomas. These leaders represented the organizations most responsible for getting civil rights laws passed. Many members of civil rights organizations felt betrayed in seeing these laws ignored.

Candidate Clarence Thomas answers reporters' questions following nomination by President Bush to the Supreme Court.

"How do you explain Judge Thomas's conduct as chairman of the EEOC?" the reporters asked. The President's answer was that the complaints were "unfounded." Realizing the reply was not an acceptable answer, the reporters persisted. The President assured them that such questions would be answered at the confirmation hearings. Then he concluded that Clarence Thomas, "seasoned now by more experience on the [court] bench, fits my description of the best man at the right time."

# Truth of the Matter

## Words of Wisdom

"The truth of the matter is we have become more interested in designer jeans and break dancing than we are in obligations and responsibilities."

Clarence Thomas's words were suddenly disturbing. A slight rustle swept through his audience, the graduating class of Savannah State College in Georgia. The date was June 9, 1985. As chairman of the EEOC as well as a former citizen of Savannah, Thomas was the guest speaker. His words of criticism had struck home, accusing the students of an all-too-common failing among them. Many were, indeed, interested in only self-indulgent lifestyles.

Earlier in his speech Thomas had cautioned:

> There is a tendency among young, upwardly mobile, intelligent minorities to forget. We forget the sweat of our forefathers. We forget the blood

of the marchers, the prayers and hope of our race. We forget who brought us into this world. We overlook those who put food in our mouths and clothes on our backs. We forget our commitment to excellence.

Many students nodded, acknowledging the truth of Thomas's words. They needed no reminder of who they were. As young African Americans they had responsibilities. In the spirit and promise of graduation, these students felt special. They were different from all those who had preceded them—or so they thought. They had listened to Clarence Thomas and took comfort in what he had to say.

> That mean, callous world out there is still very much filled with discrimination. It still holds out a different life for those who do not happen to be the right race or the right sex. It is a world in which the 'haves' continue to reap more dividends than the 'have-nots'.

These students had not shared the experiences about which Thomas spoke. But they had heard enough from their parents. They had also read enough African-American history to believe what he said was true. The students knew the challenge. And they were satisfied in accepting this responsibility.

Thomas continued:

> I stand before you as one who had the same beginning as yourselves, as one who has walked a little farther down the road, climbed a little higher up the mountain. I come back to you, who must now travel this road and climb this jagged, steep

mountain that lies ahead. I return as a messenger—a front-runner, a scout. What lies ahead of you is even tougher than what is now behind you.

## Fame and Misfortune

Thomas made this prediction in 1985. He said more than he could ever have imagined. *"What lies ahead of you is even tougher than what is now behind you."* The truth of his words were revealed in future events. Six years later Thomas would receive a nomination to the United States Supreme Court. The nomination would be an honor that was to carry Clarence Thomas to the height of fame and to the brink of disaster.

The position was in the nation's highest court. The appointment was at the President's pleasure but was also subject to the Senate's approval. This process was not without risks. The challenge was in the tough questioning by senators. Failing to gain the necessary votes was a threat, and being criticized was to be expected. But no one could have dreamt of the charge that was to prolong this hearing. The scandal that the charge created was to threaten Thomas's professional future as well as his personal life.

# Deep Are the Roots

I grew up here in Savannah. I was born not far from here (in Pin Point, Georgia). I am a child of those marshes, a son of this soil. I am a descendant of the slaves whose labors made the dark soil of the South productive. I am the great-great-grandson of a freed slave whose enslavement continued after my birth. I am the product of hatred and love—the hatred of the social and political structure which dominated the segregated, hate-filled city of my youth, and the love of some people—my mother, my grandparents, my neighbors and relatives—who said by their actions, "You can make it, but first you must endure."

As a boy Clarence Thomas never questioned where he was born. Pin Point, a seacoast community, was typical for many southern blacks. It was a place in which to survive. In the early 1950s survival meant accepting poverty and obeying segregation laws. The whites with whom blacks came in contact saw to this separation of the races. Blacks and whites often worked side by side, but only with this understanding of separatism. Whether employed in the fields or factories, blacks were expected to act as inferiors in their relationships with whites.

## Pin Point, Georgia

Outside of work, black and white lives remained separate in most communities. This was also true in Pin Point, Georgia. Situated just outside of Savannah, the town has a proud history. It was founded by freed slaves soon after the Civil War. But few outsiders had ever heard of this poor, tiny community.

The houses were old and looked makeshift. Many were in need of repair. Wood-framed and rotting, most were simply places of shelter. Running water and toilets were located outside and away from the houses, and were shared among neighboring families.

Clarence Thomas was born in 1948 in this town. He was part of the third generation of his family to live there. The house was located at the end of a narrow, sandy road. Several other families, all struggling to make ends meet, lived on the block. For most Pin Point residents, making a living meant fishing for, preparing, or selling crabs and shrimps. Clarence's parents were no exception to this tradition. They worked in the fish factory, as other family members had done before them. Their incomes maintained the family's quiet way of life.

## Series of Changes

But for the Thomases, this relatively simple life was not to last. A series of family disruptions changed everything. The changes began in 1950 with the sudden departure of the man of the house. Relocating to Philadelphia, Pennsylvania, he was never again seen nor heard from by his family. He had abandoned his wife, Leola, and three children—Clarence, his brother Myers, named after his grandfather, and sister Emma Mae. They were left to make their way as best they could.

Clarence, youngest of the children, was barely old enough to walk. His mother, still young and determined, continued to shell crabs for a living. Earning only a nickel for every pound picked, Leola did not make enough money to support the family. Struggling to survive became a way of life for the Thomases.

During the summer of 1955 their five-year struggle went from bad to worse. The family's house burned down, leaving the Thomases with nothing but the clothes on their backs. Leola had no choice but to seek public assistance. But agency officials refused her application. They claimed that her father (Clarence's grandfather, Myers Anderson) was making enough money to help out the family. Leola was denied public assistance.

## Lost in Savannah

Determined to make it on her own, Leola Thomas moved to Savannah, seven miles away. She took the two boys with her, leaving behind her daughter—Emma Mae—to live with her sister in Pin Point.

A growing industrial center, Savannah held the promise of better job opportunities. Upper-income white families were always seeking household help. Leola found cleaning homes hard work. But the wages were good—at least for an uneducated African American living in the South. However, the work kept Leola away from the family's one-room apartment. Left mostly on their own, Clarence and Myers lived on a meager diet. The one pair of shoes that each owned was for attending school. But the shoes received little use, as the boys' attendance grew less frequent. Clarence and Myers found wandering the streets and getting into mischief far more attractive than school.

After a year in Savannah, Leola Thomas saw what was becoming of her sons. She felt helpless to do anything more to help. Overwhelmed, she made a drastic decision. She sent the boys to live with their grandparents in another part of town. As Leola explained later, "I wanted Daddy to have those boys because they were boys and I couldn't handle them." Her father did just that! He brought the aimless lives of his grandsons to an abrupt end. Myers Anderson accomplished this task with a stout heart and firm hand.

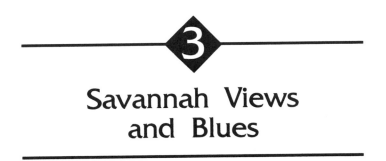

# Savannah Views
# and Blues

The Savannah in which Clarence Thomas grew up was like two cities. One was white, with neat brownstone houses, twisted oak trees, and well-kept lawns. The other was black, where dirt roads ran past run-down houses with cluttered yards. These communities, located in different parts of the same city, were worlds apart. The hope of most whites was that their lives would improve. The hope of most blacks was that their lives would not grow worse.

## History of False Hopes

Savannah has not changed greatly from the city in which Clarence Thomas was reared. The major change was in legislation outlawing segregation. Blacks and whites no longer lived in two separate worlds, but now shared the same public facilities. Yet in every other way, Savannah's African-American citizens had fewer opportunities and less of the worldly goods provided by the city. Whether today or in the 1950s, Savannah could not live up to the promise of its beginnings.

In 1733 James Oglehorpe and a group of 120 colonists founded the city of Savannah. It was Georgia's first permanent white settlement. Although the colony was using slave labor, Savannah colonists outlawed the practice. But the law was mostly ignored. Savannah was very much a product of southern colonies. The city depended upon slave labor. By 1750 the slave trade had grown into big business. And Savannah became one of the leading port cities for slave trading.

The American Revolution, declared in 1775, created false hopes among slaves. Promising freedom, the fight for independence actually had little effect on the slave trade. In the end, the defense of freedom was strictly for white Americans.

Another hope of African Americans that died a similar death was the promise of the Emancipation Proclamation. Issued by President Abraham Lincoln in 1863 during the Civil War, it freed the slaves. But the Proclamation was bitterly opposed by the Confederate states. The conflict over this document was a critical part of the war. When Union soldiers conquered the Confederate army in Georgia, General William T. Sherman led the victory. He also imposed the will of the

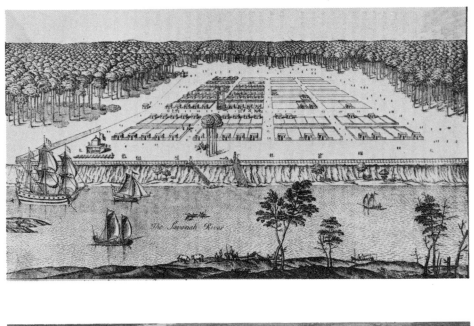

The growing city of Savannah soon after its founding in 1733 (top),
and as it appeared in the 1870s (bottom).

proclamation. Former slaves were now free to make new lives for themselves. Sherman helped prepare their way by issuing an order to right the wrong of slavery. He gave plantation lands claimed by southern whites to newly-freed blacks.

The order proved no more than noble words, however. Six months later President Lincoln was assassinated. Vice President Andrew Johnson became President. African Americans were still free by the law of the land. But for them, the promise of justice and equality died with Lincoln. One of Johnson's first acts was to overrule Sherman's order. The plantations were returned to their former owners. African Americans were once again forced to suffer the disappointment of a broken promise.

The years after the Civil War were known as the period of Reconstruction. During this time the federal government tried to force the South to change its social and political discrimination of African Americans. From 1865 to 1877 the South went through many changes. No longer slaves, African Americans were entitled to all the rights and privileges of citizens. This meant jobs in industry, positions in government, and equal status in society with white Americans. Many tried to take advantage of these opportunities. A few African Americans gained skilled jobs, government offices, and a higher social status. However, these positions were limited and proved fleeting. By the end of the century, white racism was back in force. The tradition of segregating and denying African Americans the rights of citizenship was restored.

## Period of Self-Help

Since this period of southern history, Savannah developed and became known as the "Mother City of Georgia." Besides being the state's first colonial settlement, it was one of the first planned cities in the United States. But African-American residents were nowhere included in these developments. Left to fend for themselves, they made the most of what little they had. Many worked to gain a feeling of racial identity and support. They formed chapters of the National Association for the Advancement of Colored People (NAACP) and Booker T. Washington's National Negro Business League. A few succeeded in starting several banks. In Savannah, African-American entrepreneurs helped develop a thriving business district. It included two movie theaters, variety stores, confectionery shops, and other businesses. Slowly but surely most were to fail. Few survived the Great Depression of 1929.

## Diehard Resistance

The civil rights revolution that swept through the South in the 1960s also brought changes. In 1961, for the first time, African-American children attended previously all-white schools in cities throughout Georgia. Public libraries and restaurants were no longer permitted to bar Americans because of their race.

These changes, however, were neither complete nor without resistance. Reacting to social pressure, the mayor of Savannah formed a biracial committee. Its purpose was to help put an end to the practices of segregation in the city. The committee recommended how these changes should be made. However, the mayor rejected the group's ideas and suspended the members for their suggestions.

African-American residents fought back. They organized a massive boycott of white businesses. By this time Savannah had grown into a tourist attraction. Many shops depended upon customers who visited the city. These shop owners lost money when visitors refused to cross black picket lines. By the end of the first month, local businesses lost one million dollars. The "tourist paradise" of Savannah was clearly in trouble. Business people could not afford another month's loss of income. Nor could they wait for the city's politicians to work out a solution. They decided to act in their own best interests. In 1963 local business owners worked out a plan with African-American representatives. Their agreement led to the desegregation of Savannah restaurants, theaters, hotels, and public facilities.

As one protest leader declared, "Come what may, Savannah will never be the same." He was right, although there was more than one diehard Georgia

Modern Savannah includes many buildings from its historic past.

segregationist who refused to give up. In Atlanta a major restaurant owner, Lester G. Maddox, symbolized this southern resistance. Rather than obey a federal court order to desegregate, he closed his restaurant. It was a last-ditch gesture in defense of segregation in the South.

## Alarming Results

In 1965 Martin Luther King, Jr., arrived in Savannah. This nationally famous African American had led the black civil rights movement throughout the South. His visit was to hail the ending of segregation in public facilities. Called "Jim Crow" laws, this southern tradition of racial separation was now history. But the policy change was more in the law than in the conduct of people. The law gave African Americans hope; the whites took that hope away. The results proved tragically disappointing. In a city of 140,000, more than half the population was African American. The desegregation of city schools remained largely unchanged, with mostly African-American students attending these facilities. White families continued to flee the inner city and its schools, and to create all-white suburban communities.

There were few African-American businesses, and twice as much unemployment of blacks as of whites. The few African Americans working were in the least desirable jobs and paid the lowest wages. Their income remained as little as 60 percent that of white Americans in the city. Only a handful of African Americans were officers in local government or corporations.

Hope gave way to despair, and despair led to increasing crime. The use of drugs became common, and murders increased. Black Savannah became a shame for white officials to hide, rather than a scandal to be corrected. Meanwhile, the ghetto continued to rot in poverty and neglect.

## Source of Success

Economic differences between the races remained, and with it, two separate ways of life. As African-American poverty spread, white wealth grew. The State Port of Savannah became a prime example.

One of the nation's most modern port facilities, it was bought as a quarter-master depot from the federal government after World War II. The port's business began with a simple row of warehouses built to store cotton. Since that time, the cotton industry and the business of Savannah's waterfront have greatly changed. Cotton, a leading farm product in Georgia for 100 years, now accounts for less than 2 percent of the state's agricultural income. Other industries have prospered.

Savannah's industries have become the trading center for a large farming region. Nearby sawmills ship supplies of lumber through the city each year. Other products making up Savannah's industry include wood pulp, refined sugar, fertilizer, packaged tea, petroleum

Originally built as a cotton factory, this building is now part of Savannah's scenic waterfront attraction.

products, roofing materials, ships, truck trailers, cement, and aircraft assemblies. Canneries process shrimp, crab meat, and oysters.

Savannah's historic riverfront has also been built into a tourist attraction. The city dazzles with a rebuilt tourist mecca. River Street, with nine blocks of restaurants, shops, and museums attracts many visitors. Through the cooperative efforts of city officials and private industry, Savannah has developed into Georgia's third largest city after Atlanta and Columbus. But its African-American areas remain a blight.

This is the city in which Clarence Thomas grew up. He was influenced by its history, one largely steeped in traditions. The traditions became a part of his life. In 1966, after ten years, Thomas was to leave Savannah. But he was not to forget those years. He has taken time to think about what living there has meant to him. He has also returned and seen how Savannah has changed. And he has described his impressions. They tell a lot about the man he was to become.

# The Death of "Old Man Can't"

The idea of leaving their mother was no big deal. Clarence and his brother were a team. They had been on their own for almost a year—ever since the family had moved to Savannah from Pin Point. In moving to their grandparents' house, Clarence and Myers were not going far. They were simply going to live in another part of Savannah. The change was one more adventure, something to look forward to.

But the boys could never have imagined how different the change was going to be. The good part was the house into which they moved. It was their first with an indoor bathroom. And the new living arrangement was the first time they were to enjoy eating three meals a day.

Those were the good parts of the change. The bad

part was the loss of their freedom. At least that was the way it seemed. To the boys, living with their grandparents became the worst fate of their young lives.

## Anderson's Golden Rules

Myers Anderson's words of advice hardly helped matters. And worse than his advice was his order to work instead of play. Work was a brand-new experience to the Thomas boys.

"I'm doin' this for y'all," he explained, "so y'all don't have to work for the white man, so y'all don't have to take what I had to take." He followed up with more words. But they made no more sense than the others. "There's no problem elbow grease can't solve. 'Old Man Can't' is dead. I helped bury him."

To two free-spirited boys, such words sounded crazy. They were the ravings of an old man. Angry, Clarence and Myers resisted their grandfather's ideas. Using more than one trick to escape their chores, all they got in return were old-fashioned whippings.

Myers Anderson meant what he said. There would be no more unbridled freedom. He knew the racial record of the South. Lynchings, beatings, and disappearances of young black men were still going on. He was not about to have his grandsons become victims of such racial tragedies. Allowing the boys to roam the streets was to run that risk. Anderson knew that his grandsons had a lot to learn. And he also knew that he had a lot of teaching and persuading to do.

Clarence Thomas was to become a product of his grandfather's words. "Man ain't got no business on relief as long as he can work." The "relief" his grandfather meant was "doing nothing." As a living example, Myers Anderson was a man doing *something*. He was not content to exist as just another illiterate black man. He had survived southern segregation with dignity and determination. These qualities served him well. Myers Anderson developed his own business. His success became a role model for Clarence Thomas.

## All Work and No Play

Short and powerfully built, Myers Anderson demanded no less of himself than he did of others. He worked seven days a week, collecting and delivering ice, wood, and cinderblocks. He also worked in real estate. Through such buying and selling, he made a good living. Myers Anderson had no time for play. His example must have alarmed two young boys whose way of life was dead-set against such labors.

Among the many changes for Clarence and Myers was better school attendance, which went from sometimes to all the time. Their grandfather would have it no other way. Myers Anderson was a strong believer in education. He insisted that the boys regularly attend school. Anderson also decided that their attendance was not to be at any old black school. He chose a Catholic school run by strict Irish nuns. The tuition, at thirty dollars per year, was a sacrifice he could ill afford. But as a devout Catholic, Anderson felt the money was well spent. The sisters at the school were just what his grandsons needed. They taught the boys in the same way he did—by example. The lesson being taught was the rewards of hard work.

Catholic school marked the real beginning of the Thomas boys' formal education. It also marked the beginning of their discipline. Their education included learning inside as well as outside of the classroom. Soon, visiting the library became a regular recreational activity. Their discipline included a strict routine in their daily lives. School was only part of the day's activities. At home personal chores waited to be completed.

The after-school routine became set. The boys headed straight for home and changed into their work clothes. Then they worked in and around the house for the next six hours. These chores included tending to chickens, pigs, and cows as well as cleaning the house and yard. Added to these duties were special chores, including painting, roofing, plumbing, and general fixing. Finally, the boys were responsible for helping their grandfather in his work. This meant maintaining his oil and ice trucks, and helping him make deliveries throughout the neighborhood.

After their work was done, the Thomas boys were

Clarence Thomas (left) and companion preparing to serve as altar boys in a local church service.

free. By now, however, it was nearly nine o'clock at night. They could spend the few remaining hours before bed to do what they pleased. Clarence made the most of his free hours, using the time to dash to the local library. He was later to recall this experience. "I used to run to the library to flip through the pages and dream." The dream was of a better future. The way for making his dream come true was through books and study.

## Lessons in Southern Exposure

Myers Anderson lacked an education, but not willpower. Using his will, he improved himself and the conditions of his people. He voted regularly and was active in the local chapter of the NAACP. This nationally famous African-American civil rights organization was involved in racial projects. Its members worked for voter registration and participated in sit-ins—activities that highlighted the 1960s. During this period the city experienced a 16-month boycott of its main shopping area.

On Sunday afternoons Clarence sometimes accompanied his grandfather to NAACP meetings. And on more than one occasion, Myers Anderson would show off his grandson. He would have Clarence read his report card aloud. These occasions were for all to learn of the boy's impressive school grades.

Myers Anderson decided that he wanted the best for his promising grandson, Clarence. That meant St. John

Vianney Minor Seminary, an all-white Catholic boarding school. By this time, in 1960, racial segregation was still being practiced. But the South was beginning to change. Myers Anderson exercised his legal right to have Clarence apply to the all-white school. And his grandson was admitted to the seminary without incident.

Clarence proceeded to make excellent school grades. He also became a star quarterback on the school's football team. His grandfather saw these accomplishments as living proof that black people were as good as white people. And he bragged that his grandson would one day become a priest.

## Stranger and Alone

But Clarence's experiences as a seminary student were not happy times. Not only was this his first time living around whites, but this was also his first time to experience racism firsthand. Clarence saw how many possessions whites had, and realized how much better off they were than most blacks. Much as he tried to fit in with the other students, the youngster was mostly ignored. He was also made to feel different. In class Clarence worked hard to excel, learning to speak perfectly and act properly. But none of these accomplishments mattered outside of class. Whether attending the theater, eating in a restaurant, or simply socializing, his treatment was the same. Schoolmates

Clarence Thomas at study with a classmate, one of his few high school friends.

excluded him from their activities. They ignored Clarence and made him feel as though he did not exist.

When he was noticed, it was mostly as the butt of racial jokes. After lights out, a standard remark was spoken. "Smile, Clarence, so we can see you!" And, each time, everyone laughed. Not one person ever spoke up in his defense. Clarence could not help himself. He compared this treatment with the image his grandfather had created of the Catholic Church. The beauty of the religion contrasted the ugliness of some of its members.

Clarence Thomas graduated from the seminary. But he came away with bitter feelings. Nothing he could do would make him accepted by white people. The only thing a black person could do was to achieve. Clarence Thomas would become the living proof: he would achieve. Enrolling at Immaculate Conception Seminary in Missouri was a first step. The move was planned to continue his training for the priesthood. But he stayed for only eight months. The assassination of Martin Luther King, Jr., on April 4, 1968 destroyed this dream.

News of the shooting had just been reported. For the moment, no one knew anything more. Was the civil rights leader dead or alive? That day in April 1968, Thomas was entering a classroom. He overheard one of the white students wish the black minister's death. "I hope like hell he dies," the student said. This vicious remark was the last straw to Clarence's religious calling. The words shattered his trust in and devotion to the

Clarence Thomas as he appears in his high school yearbook.

church. Suddenly he was alone. This feeling was impressed on him by the whites with whom he had lived and studied. The words also made a lie of his grandfather's teachings, and his grandfather was a man whom he worshipped. Clarence Thomas recovered from this shock. No longer a boy, he became his own man. He was now ready to make a future for himself, and in his own way.

# Way to Go

His experience at the seminary taught him a lesson. Clarence Thomas decided that he was no longer willing to continue his religious studies. Life in religious service was not for him. But deciding on what he did want to do was something else. He had no answer for this problem. The young man had yet to learn who he was. And he had yet to figure out how he wanted to spend his life.

## Plan of Action

Thomas did know his first order of business, which was to get away from the South's racism. He thought that this change would offer a real opportunity. There must be a place in America, he thought, where an African American could be judged as a person rather than as an object. He believed he should be judged by the quality of his work rather than the color of his skin. He only had to find the right place and the right college. Thomas searched for one that would recognize and build on his Catholic training. At the urging of one of his Savannah nuns, he applied to Holy Cross in Worcester, Massachusetts. The college held the promise of serving his needs.

Finding tuition became the next challenge. College fees amounted to thousands of dollars. Scholarships, monies set aside to assist students, offered the best possibility. All scholarships required special qualifications. Many were being offered in the 1970s, one type of which was for minority students. Clarence Thomas qualified for this type of scholarship and was off to a promising start.

However, none of these scholarships fully covered college expenses. So Thomas applied for as many as he could find. Together with various grants, loans, and the college's work-study program, he was able to register. Once enrolled as a full-time student, Thomas began a brand-new life.

## Campus Woes

Holy Cross was a new experience for Clarence Thomas. The overwhelmingly white campus was situated on a hill overlooking the grim-looking factory town. Both the buildings and the people were different from the warm familiar sights of the South. These differences hardly mattered, though. Thomas was a young black southerner attending a northern white school. Adjusting to these differences kept him busy. Plus, there were the demands of his schoolwork, and the responsibilities he felt. Besides excelling in his academic subjects, Thomas maintained a full extracurricular schedule of activities. He ran on the track team, participated in touch football and pickup basketball games, and was active socially. He helped found the Black Student Union, serving as its first treasurer and writing its constitution. He was also involved in several civil rights protests in Worcester.

Thomas became a rebel with a cause. He wore a goatee, army fatigues, combat boots, and displayed a poster of Malcolm X in his dormitory room. At the same time he also saw it as his duty to work in the black community. He became involved in the free breakfast program organized for Worcester's black schoolchildren. Many of them had been attending school without breakfast. As a result they were ill-prepared to learn. Hot meals started off their day right. The program was also a first step for improving their classroom performance.

Thomas became a student volunteer in the program. One morning a week he rose at dawn to serve breakfast to the poor children in a church basement in Worcester. He also tutored black students living in the Worcester community.

## Experience as Teacher

Thomas learned a lot from his experiences in Massachusetts. He learned that Worcester was not all that different from the South. Many racial incidents reminded him of this fact. The difference was that the racism was now more subtle. But this difference did not help; it only made the insults all the more offensive.

From these experiences, and what he read, Thomas came to a conclusion. The only way for African-American people to improve their lives was to help themselves. They had to change the conditions creating their problems. He had read about the Black Panthers, an organization of militant black Americans. Members of this group had developed a self-help program. And they demonstrated how it could work. At this time, in the early 1970s, the Black Panthers were based in Oakland, California. There they ran a free food program, health clinic, and elementary school in the local African-American community. The success of these programs attracted national publicity. Thomas was impressed. He saw these programs as dramatic examples of how African Americans could improve their lives: by doing things for themselves wherever possible.

## Root of All Evil

But sometimes self-help is at the expense of other people. Thomas felt that Holy Cross was guilty of exploiting black South Africans by making corporate investments in South African companies.

The fact is that colleges operate very much like companies. They have to make money to stay in business. Income from students' tuitions is not enough to cover their expenses. Colleges have to invest money in profit-making companies. In turn, the colleges share the profits with their investors. Holy Cross was one such college.

South African industries were very profitable for their investors. Doing business with South African companies was simply good business—everybody involved made money. Everybody except the poor unskilled workers of South Africa, most of whom were black. They were working at the lowest wages and under the worst conditions. They were also victims of the worst racial discrimination and segregation in the world. This system was known as apartheid. For Holy Cross to do business with South Africa was to profit at the expense of people, particularly black people. Thomas protested with other students in staging a walkout at the college.

## Time Out

For all his involvement in civic activities, Thomas found time for social activities as well. There were flirtations with members of the opposite sex. But nothing serious developed until his senior year when he started dating Kathy Ambush. A native of Worcester, she was attending a nearby college when they met. They were married on June 5, 1971—the day after Thomas's graduation from Holy Cross.

The young couple's married life was frequently tested. Clarence had unusual ambitions that created unusual demands. For, by this time, he had come to a critical decision. He felt his primary responsibility was for the welfare of African-American people. And the most effective way to improve their welfare was through the study of law. Thomas received this opportunity from Yale University. Young, disadvantaged African Americans with outstanding school grades were actively being recruited for the Yale Law School. Thomas was a natural candidate, and his application to Yale was accepted.

Thomas also came to understand that African Americans had to do more for themselves. His grandfather had taught him this lesson, and his experiences at Holy Cross had provided him with proof. He felt the best place to start was by personal example. This meant more than passing examinations; it meant excelling. And Thomas did excel, managing to maintain a near-perfect academic record. He was also active outside the classroom. Black students looked to him for leadership, while black citizens of the community welcomed him for his volunteer work. Thomas accepted these roles as obligations. And he dedicated himself to making the most of them.

Divinity School, one of many buildings on the Yale University campus where Clarence Thomas attended law school.

## Making the Grade

Despite his generally successful experiences at Yale, Thomas was in conflict with himself. His confusion was of the boy he had been with the man he had become. He continued his work in the black community. He joined the New Haven Legal Assistance Program. And he involved himself in other community programs. These activities kept him busy, and they also attracted attention to him.

Yale's African-American law students were having a problem. They wanted more African Americans enrolled. School officials thought they were doing enough. The students asked Thomas to lead a protest against the school's policy. Thomas refused, arguing that many African-American students never graduated. These dropouts often were the children of poor families. Most of those who did graduate were the offspring of doctors, lawyers, teachers, and other professionals.

The product of a poor uneducated family, Thomas felt removed from the students who wanted to protest. Their problem was strictly their own. He could not justify leading such a protest, whose effect would be more law degrees for middle-class African Americans. As he explained:

> If quotas help you, fine. If they make your life wonderful, fine. If they get you a BMW or Mercedes [luxury automobiles] say that is why you want quotas. Man, quotas are for the black middle class. But look at what's happening to the masses.

Those are my people. They are just where they
were before any of these policies.

Thomas had trouble with the role of a political
activist. He made his remarks as a student, refusing to set
himself apart as an African-American student. Wanting
no special favors, he sat in the back of the classroom to
avoid notice. He also stayed clear of courses dealing with
social issues. Instead, Thomas studied the laws of tax,
legal accounting, antitrust, and property. This was his
way of responding to the "monkey on my back."

The "monkey" was his belief about what his white
classmates thought. They thought African-American
students received special treatment, being admitted to
Yale simply to satisfy the school's racial quota. They
believed African Americans were never admitted for their
academic qualifications. Thomas was determined to
expose this notion as a myth.

## Lasting Impression

In 1974 Thomas graduated from Yale Law School. Also
in this year his wife, Kathy, gave birth to their son,
Jamal. These blessings made Thomas more confident.
Yet he became more a loner than ever before. He had
passed his courses with honors. He had competed
successfully with the best white minds. And he had
avoided calling attention to his race. No one could say
he had used his color for personal gain. But in this effort,

51

he had become a stranger—as much to himself as to his race.

Clarence Thomas felt he owed no one for his success. He owed Yale least of all. True, the law school had accepted an African American from a poor family. But Thomas felt this fact was beside the point. "I don't think black people are indebted to anybody for anything," he has said. "Nobody has done us any favors in this country, buddy. All they [whites] did was stop stopping us." Clarence Thomas was declaring himself a living example. He had made it on his own, and he was claiming all the credit.

# One of a Kind

Graduates of Yale Law School are generally treated as special people. Their reputation is of above-average lawyers. As a result, they are ready and waiting for successful careers. Big companies offer its graduates special opportunities. In the 1970s, companies sent representatives to the Yale campus where they then competed for these trained professionals. The young men and women, in turn, picked among the job offers, considering only the ones that looked the most promising.

## Special Choice

Thomas was among the graduates given this opportunity. Strictly through his own choice, he had specialized in tax law. This field deals with legal interpretations rather than people, especially people of color. Clarence Thomas would not be accused of being an African-American lawyer catering to the rights of African-American people.

He was wrong, however. His choice in law hardly mattered. What mattered was the color of his skin. As an African American, Thomas's law career was assumed. Representatives of white law firms considered him for only one kind of law. It was for the welfare of African American people rather than the interests of white corporations.

This was Thomas's experience even when he explained the courses he had taken. Corporate representatives insisted that they knew what was in his best interest. They did not have to explain what they meant. Laws protecting the rights of the disadvantaged was the only law for a black lawyer.

Thomas was disgusted. For strangers to assume that they knew what was best for him was an insult. He stormed out of more than one interview. "I went to law school to be a lawyer, not a social worker," he has since complained. "If I want to be a social worker, I'll do it on my own time."

His white friends were surprised to learn of Thomas's experience. None of them had been treated this way, nor could they understand why a fellow classmate had been. Thomas understood: he knew that nothing had changed. The reaction of the recruiters was the way he had been made to feel all through his schooling. He was different, all right—and all because of his color. There was but one interview in which he was made to feel like a lawyer and nothing more. It was also his last, since he took the job. The position was as an assistant attorney general in Missouri. His boss, John Danforth, was Missouri's attorney general. The work proved to Thomas's liking. As he was later to report, "Danforth ignored the hell out of me." This left Thomas free to do his own thing.

## Prime Time Opportunities

The work dealt with a variety of cases, ranging from tax to criminal law. The job proved a three-year learning experience. His boss, meanwhile, was making political gains. In 1977 Danforth decided to run for the United States Senate. Vacating his position as attorney general, Danforth ran as Missouri's Republican candidate and won. The office of U.S. Senator required that he move to Washington, D.C. As part of the now departing Danforth administration, Thomas knew it was also his time to move on.

He took a position in the legal department of Monsanto Company, a manufacturer of soaps and cosmetics. After two years with the company, Thomas was invited to Washington, D.C. His appointment was as Senator Danforth's legislative assistant, a position he held from 1979 to 1981. Then in 1981 President Ronald Reagan named him for the position of Assistant

Secretary for Civil Rights. The office was in the United States Department of Education. Clarence Thomas was now a favored figure in the Republican administration—a man to watch. A year later he was once again named by the President. This time the appointment was to the position of chairman of the Equal Employment Opportunity Commission.

## Taking Office

The commission was created in 1964 for the purpose of stopping discrimination in the workplace. Employees now had an official government agency to which to take their complaints. The office had the authority to protect workers' civil rights on the job. These rights included protection against discrimination on the basis of race, sex, color, religion, and national origin.

EEOC's power was limited to investigating employee charges. A five-member commission reviewed every case recommended by the agency. Those cases approved were then acted upon by commission officials. They would try to settle with the employer. That failing, a lawsuit was then filed against the company.

Heading such an important agency was a challenge. Clarence Thomas knew this all too well. But he could not have imagined how the challenges would begin.

The first challenge was to gain admittance to his office. On Thomas's first day, he had to convince the guard of whom he was. Once inside his office, he faced a massive oak desk. But he noticed that it had no chair—nor was one anywhere in sight. Though he could not know at the time, the desk was like the agency; it was most impressive. The missing chair was like the agency's organization; it was sadly lacking.

Thomas quickly ordered a chair for himself. Then he ordered two flags. One was the stars and bars of the state of Georgia. The other he had specially made. It was embroidered with the words "Don't Tread on Me." The message was a warning to all those having business with the EEOC. Clarence Thomas intended to run the agency his way.

## Comrade in Arms

The President's appointment was not a popular one. This was especially true among EEOC staff members. President Reagan had shown little understanding of or interest in African Americans. And he had done nothing for their needs. Why should he be expected to select a chairman who would oppose his views? Black or white, Clarence Thomas was seen as a man not to be trusted. EEOC staff members worried about their new boss. They wondered whether he really believed in the agency's mission.

They did not have long to wait. Thomas quickly settled into his new job. And, just as quickly, he issued his first order. It was for his staff to do better. He made it clear that the agency needed the best they had to offer.

He went on to warn that tough times were ahead. But he insisted that, together, they could build an agency of which they could all feel proud.

The men and women who worked for Thomas were to learn the truth of his words. The new chairman was a man who meant what he said. He established personal contacts with staff members, visiting the finance section on a regular basis. These visits were not to observe, but to work with and help staff members complete their assignments. Good working relationships developed, and so did staff loyalty. This result was due as much to the man Clarence Thomas was as to the new policies he established.

## Personal Policies

Thomas's eight years at the EEOC were difficult, almost from the start. The first problem was the agency's size. Overseeing 3,100 employees and forty-eight local offices was an awesome responsibility. The second was the need to do something about organizing the agency.

Another problem was the large case load of complaints. Thomas questioned many of these cases. Most of the cases he questioned dealt with class-action suits. These were cases in which members of a particular group charged a company with discrimination. Such cases were now being rejected. Thomas had long decided that unfair treatment meant unfair treatment of an individual. It did not mean of a group. His interpretation greatly reduced the backlog of agency cases. This policy also reduced the number of people benefitting from the agency.

Thomas defended this change in agency policy. He argued:

> . . . the protection of *individual* rights is what this nation is all about—or should be all about. Not group rights, but individual rights. Affirmative action addresses groups, and assumes that blacks can't perform as well as whites, that educated blacks can't compete with whites.

Thomas further insisted that "affirmative action does nothing for the vast majority of poor and uneducated African Americans. They remain out of work and out of hope."

His explanation failed to satisfy his critics. Civil rights groups were especially upset. They saw affirmative action as a necessary step for African Americans to gain fair treatment in the workplace. It was the only way to make up for past practices of racial discrimination. They insisted that without class-action suits there would be no safeguard for minorities in the workplace. Minorities would continue to be the last hired at the lowest jobs for the least pay. And they would continue to be the first to be laid off during a cutback.

The feud between Thomas and civil rights groups grew. It was something Thomas said he was prepared to live with. What he could not have imagined was the hardship this decision would have on his private life.

Clarence Thomas and his mother, Leola Williams, enjoy the privacy of home and escape from the limelight of the nation's capital.

In 1984 he divorced. The fact was neither sudden nor painless. There were the difficulties of disagreements, the pain of legal proceedings, and finally, the added burden of a single father raising a ten-year-old boy. And, all the while, there were the demands of his job. Besides tending to numerous administrative details, there were countless meetings and travel to numerous conferences.

While attending an affirmative action conference in New York City in 1986 Thomas met Virginia Lamp. A 34-year-old Labor Department lawyer, she found herself in agreement with his views on civil rights and enjoying his company. Their friendship blossomed, and they were married a year later.

Thomas's stand on civil rights was also a position from which he was to benefit. In 1989 he was named for the Washington, D.C., Court of Appeals. The nomination was opposed by most civil rights groups. But they could not block Thomas's appointment to this second-highest court in the nation.

# The Supreme Court

"The judicial power of the United States shall be vested in one supreme court, and in such inferior courts as the Congress may from time to time ordain and establish."

This is Article III of the U.S. Constitution, written in 1787 during the Constitutional Convention. Leading statesmen from the former thirteen colonies had gathered in Philadelphia. Their purpose was to form a national government. They succeeded in creating an executive and legislative branch of government. George Washington was later named to fill the executive office, becoming the nation's first President.

The legislative office was to be made up of senators and representatives. Each state was to elect two senators. The number of representatives was dependent on the population in each state.

The judiciary branch had to wait until the legislators were in office. It was the legislators' duty to organize this branch of government. Carrying out this responsibility took time, delaying the start of the Supreme Court until February 1, 1790.

## Powers of the Court

In 1831 a famous French historian named Alexis de Tocqueville visited the United States. After studying this new government, he came to a conclusion: the Supreme Court was its most powerful branch. As he explained, the power of the President was limited by the Constitution. The power of Congress was limited by the short terms served by its members. But members of the Supreme Court were in office for life. If they were ill-chosen, the nation could be doomed. Tocqueville warned, "The Union may be plunged into anarchy or civil war."

As written in the Constitution, the basic duty of the Supreme Court is to uphold the laws. The Court interprets the laws for federal, state, and local governments. These laws are recognized and acted upon by all other courts. In this way the Supreme Court helps guarantee equal justice to all Americans.

## Justices of the Court

Members of the court are nominated by the President. They are then voted on by members of the Senate. A majority of senators must vote their approval before the nominee can be sworn in as an associate justice. Barring any misdeed, a justice can hold this office for life. This clause protects court members from political influences, making justices independent of both public opinion and lawmakers.

Beyond these requirements is the number of Supreme Court justices. This number has changed several times. The final change to nine members came in 1869, and called for a chief justice and eight associate justices. The Constitution has no qualifications for the office. But all members have had some legal training and experience in law. And most court justices have been judges, lawyers, law teachers, or government officials.

The Supreme Court helps resolve national problems. Many are the most important and controversial issues in the United States. Among these problems are civil rights—especially of women and minorities— environmental protection, and abortion rights.

The decisions of the Supreme Court establish legal rules within the government. All public officials as well as the rest of Americans are bound by the court's decisions. This includes owners and officers in private companies as well as private citizens. Claims of legal violations are also subject to Supreme Court action and rulings. The rulings may include, for example, mandating practices in the workplace to ensure that workers breathe clean air. Once the Supreme Court decides an issue, various government agencies must see that it is obeyed.

## Increasing Case Loads

The Supreme Court is very much like the American Constitution. Its structure and purpose have remained unchanged for almost two hundred years. Yet the court has adjusted to the nation's growing problems. As the problems have increased, so has the court's case load. Between 1958 and 1962, for example, these cases totaled three times as many as between 1948 and 1952. And in the 1980s that number doubled again. Today the court's case load is well over 5,000 per year, and climbing.

There are many reasons for this increase. With the growth in population, crimes have grown even faster. A more informed public has also shown an increased willingness to take action. Such factors have helped increase public demands for Supreme Court decisions.

## Matter of Procedure

It is the right of every citizen to take a case to court. The case is then heard in a local court. If the person is not satisfied with the court's verdict, he or she can take the case to a higher court. This is at the state or district level. If still not satisfied, the person may, level by level, take the case to the Supreme Court. This court then decides whether to hear the case. The chance, however, is not likely. The Supreme Court has refused to hear over 90 percent of the cases it receives. Then the lower court's decision stands. If the Supreme Court accepts the case, it has a decision to make. The court must decide on which issue in the case it will deal. Or it may decide to deal with the case as presented.

In hearing a case the justices consider written and oral arguments. These arguments are presented by lawyers and lay people on either side of the issue. During these presentations justices are free to interrupt and to ask questions. After the hearing, they discuss the case in conference. The chief justice begins the discussion, and the associate justices give their opinions. They do this in order of seniority, with those serving longest in the court going first. The justices then vote in reverse order of their seniority. This time those serving the shortest time go first. Cases are decided by majority vote. If a tie occurs, the lower court decision is left standing. The parties involved in the case have no further appeal.

## Court in Session

If the chief justice has voted with the majority, he selects a justice to write the opinion of the court. This opinion is called the majority opinion. If the chief justice has not voted with the majority, the senior justice of the majority vote assigns the opinion. A justice who disagrees with the majority opinion may write a dissenting opinion. And a justice who agrees with the majority opinion may write a concurring opinion. Authors of the opinions announce them in public sessions.

The time in which the court is in session is called a "term." It begins the first Monday in October. Justices remain in session until the beginning of the next term one year later. Most of the term is divided into "sittings." These last approximately two weeks with two-week breaks. During these sittings the justices meet and decide on the cases waiting to be heard.

Justices spend some time away from Washington, D.C., during the summer. But they continue reviewing requests for court hearings. They also involve lower court justices for special action. On occasion the court must hold a special summer hearing on an urgent case. At the end of summer the cycle begins again.

## Behind Closed Doors

A Supreme Court justice's workday is officially from 10:00 A.M. until 3:00 P.M. But sometimes there is earlier business. On Mondays the court announces the business conducted the preceding Friday. These announcements include the cases dropped. The court generally hears four cases in a session. Each side is given about a half hour to present its case.

The remainder of the justices' time is devoted to their individual work. This includes research on petitions for hearings and reviews of cases scheduled for argument.

Additional work includes the writing of opinions and reactions to other justices' opinions.

## Nine "Kingdoms" of Justice

Each Supreme Court justice has a staff of about 320 people. One court secretary described this operation as "nine separate kingdoms." More than half of these staff members serve under the marshall of the court. Their responsibility is to assist the marshall in carrying out the orders of the court. About thirty staff members work for the clerk of the court. They are responsible for processing all the cases that come to the court. The reporter is responsible for the official record. This person supervises the preparation of the court's decisions.

Each justice is served by secretaries and law clerks. The law clerks are the most important members of the staff. In 1988 seven of the justices employed four clerks each. Two justices chose to use three clerks each. The clerks are usually recent law school graduates. They also tend to be the best students from the best law schools.

Clerks spend most of their time studying the lower court cases submitted for Supreme Court hearing. They then summarize this information for the justices. Clerks also help with the research. This information is used as a basis for deciding cases. Many justices also have their clerks help in writing drafts of their opinions. Clerks usually serve a justice for one year. After leaving the court, they often go on to successful careers of their own.

## Pressuring for Just Opinions

Justices also work together on opinions. When a justice feels strongly about a case, that justice will attempt to influence other justices. These discussions account for the shifting of votes and court decisions. Through discussion, a justice may change his or her opinion about a case. This is all part of the court's decision-making process. Most often the court's opinion is the result of discussions. The justice assigned to the case debates with other members of the court. The final opinion is sometimes quite different from the original opinion. This is true even when the same justice has written both opinions.

History has also shown changes in the court's legal interpretations. Many of these changes started with special-interest groups. Some concerns of these groups, such as the protection of human rights and liberties, have expanded to include all Americans. In demonstrating their concerns, special-interest groups pressure the thinking of the court.

# A Pledge of Allegiance

The history of the Supreme Court represents the nation's pride and prejudice. The pride involves its legal power, since members of the court decide the law of the land. The prejudice involves some of its decisions. One example of prejudice is 'in the court's history. The Supreme Court did not include an African American as a member until 1967, when Thurgood Marshall was confirmed. Nor did it accept its first female justice until 1981, when Sandra Day O'Conner was confirmed.

## Cases in Point

Further examples of the court's prejudice are found in decisions that reflected America's racial attitudes at the time. For example, in the 1800s, many rich and powerful white Americans found it in their interest to maintain slavery. In 1842 the court ruled itself powerless to overturn the Fugitive Slave Law. This law gave southern whites the right to recapture runaway slaves in "free" (northern) states. The Dred Scott decision in 1857 ruled against African Americans. The court said that African Americans "had no rights which the white man was bound to respect." That included the right to their freedom from slavery.

In 1883 the Supreme Court approved the segregation of African Americans in all states. This meant that black people were denied the right to use the same public facilities as whites.

Then in 1896 the Supreme Court declared "separate but equal" laws constitutional. Whites continued to have exclusive use of public facilities, separate and apart from blacks. In actual fact, separate meant unequal. African Americans were left with less.

## Making Amends

The Supreme Court did not begin abolishing racially prejudiced laws until 1915. One of these rulings was against the grandfather clause. This law prevented a man from voting unless his grandfather had voted. Since slaves had not been considered citizens, they had no vote. Nor could African Americans born after slavery have grandfathers who had voted. As a result black people could not qualify to vote. The court ruled this law illegal.

Until 1938, African-American students were barred from attending white colleges in the South. The court ruled that African-American students had the right to enter state colleges. Then, slowly, the court began changing other racial laws. Southern whites resisted. Many simply ignored these new laws, while others used excuses. Challenged by the tricks of southern racism, the court grew impatient. It enlisted the aid of federal marshalls to enforce their rulings. Within three years, more than a million African Americans in the Deep South had registered to vote.

In 1954 the Supreme Court declared another law unconstitutional. It ruled that "separate but equal schools" for blacks and whites were, in fact, unequal. All segregated schools in America were to be integrated with "all deliberate speed." However, this change proved deliberately slow. Still, it was a beginning. Attending "white" schools meant improved education and educational facilities for African-American children. Clarence Thomas became one of the thousands to benefit.

## Candidate and Controversy

The nomination of Clarence Thomas to the Supreme Court was controversial. At forty-three years of age, he was considered by many as too inexperienced to serve on the nation's highest court. But his age and experience were the least of the problems he represented. His race was the underlying issue. As an African American, he was expected by civil rights groups to represent their cause. This meant favoring civil rights laws and being a member of the Democratic Party. Clarence Thomas was neither a Democrat nor did he believe in the African-American agenda of civil rights organizations. Being a Republican and a conservative caused many African Americans to wonder about him. How could Clarence Thomas be his own man instead of a tool to be used by the white establishment?

## Trial and Ordeal

The Thomas hearings addressed some of these issues and many more points of law and order. And the court nominee responded to these questions in a way that promised his approval to serve in the court. Then, quietly at first, a rumor grew that drew the interest of the public and attention of the Senate Judiciary Committee. For Thomas, the hearings took a dramatic turn for the worse.

The rumor was that Clarence Thomas had taken unfair and uninvited advantage of a woman with whom he had worked while heading the EEOC. A public charge of sexual harassment was brought against Thomas by Anita F. Hill. A law professor at the University of Oklahoma, Hill's accusations were too serious to be dismissed. Members of the Senate hearing committee

Clarence Thomas testifying at his confirmation hearings.

decided they needed to investigate the charge. They called for a recess of the hearings.

Both Hill and Thomas were asked to explain their relationship. Their statements were closely questioned for several days by committee members, and the proceedings were nationally televised. Supporters of both Thomas and Hill were disturbed by the amount of questions asked and the length of time the hearings consumed. They sympathized with the two star witnesses over the toll the proceedings were taking on them. In the end the hearings did not function as a court trial, but an investigation. They neither acquitted nor convicted Thomas, and neither proved nor disproved Hill's charges.

A few days after the hearings, the U.S. Senate in a close vote approved the appointment of Clarence Thomas to the Supreme Court. Advocates of women's rights were outraged. They felt that a man accused of sexual harassment should not be appointed to the court. Most civil rights groups were equally upset. They objected to the choice of a conservative African American to represent them on the court.

However, Thomas also had many supporters. They claimed that he had proved himself during the trial as an extremely capable man. And they believed his public record had proved him a fully qualified professional. They were thrilled over his appointment and the success they felt he would be as an associate justice.

Wife Virginia and son Jamal in rapt attention during Clarence
Thomas' Supreme Court confirmation hearings.

## Pomp and Circumstance

October 18, 1991 was a bright and sunny day. About 1,000 friends and family members had come to share in the swearing in of the court's newest member, its 106th justice in the nation's history. They were gathered on the South Lawn of the White House, the official home of the President. The occasion was doubly gratifying for Thomas. No one had traveled a longer, bumpier road to achieve this goal. And only one other African American, Thurgood Marshall, had served in this most powerful court in the United States. Some of the guests were from Thomas's hometown in Pin Point, Georgia. Others had served with Thomas in government agencies. Most were friends, former colleagues, and simply admirers. A few had testified at his Senate confirmation hearings. Washington officials who had worked with Thomas or on his behalf at one time or another were also present.

Their smiles expressed the happiness they felt for Clarence Thomas and his family. And the equally happy smiles of Thomas' family expressed their thanks. Family members included wife Virginia, son Jamal, mother Leola Williams, sister Emma Mae Martin, and brother Myers, among other relatives.

All had shared the pain of his confirmation. They listened as the President said, "Clarence Thomas has endured America at its worst. And he's answered with America at its best." Many of the guests nodded their heads in agreement.

Newly named member of the Supreme Court, Clarence Thomas gives thumbs up approval in company with (from left to right) son Jamal Thomas, mother Leola Williams, and stepfather Mr. Williams.

Appointment of Clarence Thomas to the Supreme Court occasions a happy reunion of family members (from left to right) wife Virginia, mother Leola Williams, and sister Emma Mae.

Now, with hundreds of well-wishers looking on, Clarence Thomas was about to be sworn in. The ceremony marked the end of a long difficult period in his life. It also marked the beginning of a promising future. Thomas stood ready and waiting. Beside him was his wife, holding the Bible on which he was to take the oath of office. Thomas gazed out at his audience. His expression, mostly serious, would be briefly interrupted by a smile that revealed his true feelings.

## Paying Homage

After taking the oath, Thomas was invited to say a few words. He began by referring to the Senate hearings.

> Since that bright, sunny day in Kennebunkport, July 1, there have been many difficult days as we all went through the confirmation battle, and I mean we all. But on this sunny day in October, at the White House, there is joy. Joy in the morning.

Thomas had neither the time nor the interest in reliving the past. He mentioned it only as "brutal, just brutal." When Anita Hill went public with her charges, Thomas reportedly had exclaimed to his wife, "That's it! They can have it! I give up!" But, he did not give up. In fighting back, he was encouraged by his wife. And he was supported by his family, the understanding of his friends, and the strength of his faith.

Clarence Thomas survived. More than that, he triumphed. He had reason to celebrate. Instead, he looked mostly grateful, as though overwhelmed by the

Clarence Thomas sharing fond memories with his favorite teacher.

experience and the many people to whom he felt indebted. There were those who had shared in his journey from Pin Point, Georgia, to the Supreme Court. And there was his grandfather who had taught him about life, and the nuns who had taught him in school. All had helped him to achieve this exalted honor. All had become a very special part of his life.

# The Judge and
# His Jury

The Supreme Court meets in a large, attractive, marble building. Like other government buildings in Washington, D.C., it appears removed from the problems of people. But that is only from the outside. Inside, the Supreme Court building is different. The inner chamber includes a thick roll book called a docket. It summarizes the cases awaiting action by the court. The length of the list is impressive. The number of cases suggests how involved the court is in the nation's legal problems.

The court chamber is where the justices meet. It is quiet and rich looking. When the justices are in attendance, the atmosphere of the room grows hushed, and the session becomes a historic event. Three days a week, after taking his seat, Chief Justice William H. Rehnquist welcomes any

The historic Supreme Court building in Washington, D.C.

The court room of the Supreme Court, scene of national law-making decisions.

new lawyers to the court. Then the hearings begin, and the justices listen as the lawyers present their cases.

## Court in Session

Supreme Court justices are like teachers. The laws written by Congress are test papers. The justices try to figure out what these legislators meant in writing their new laws. Drafts of laws are not always clearly written. And the justices must understand a law's meaning before they can decide whether it is constitutional or not.

Clarence Thomas, the latest member to join this decision-making body, is also the most closely watched. Many are comforted by his political record. But many more are not. Some see his personal life as a fairy tale. It is, indeed, an American dream come true. Others see his life as a tragedy. It is of a man who has sold his soul to the devil. These conflicting impressions create a confusing image.

The fact that he is a conservative African American makes Thomas different and strangely alone. These facts also raise many questions. Who is Clarence Thomas? What does he bring to the court? What can be expected of him? What in his past will most influence his future decisions? To question the facts of his life is to guess at Clarence Thomas's professional future.

Clarence Thomas signs in his first day on the job under the watchful eyes of Chief Justice Rehnquist, with associate justices.

## Fair Play

There was a period in his childhood before living with his grandfather when things were different. Clarence Thomas had more time than he knew what to do with. He was not yet of a mind to make anything of himself. Instead, having a good time was what he was all about.

One popular pastime he enjoyed was playing cards. He played for fun and profit. The fun came from simply the joy of the game, while the profit came from winning the pot of pennies. Thomas well remembers the time. The lesson he learned from playing cards is a story he loves to tell.

He was playing blackjack with some boys on the back porch of a neighbor's house. As they played, one boy kept winning. Thomas finally figured out how. The boy was cheating with marked cards. Thomas challenged him, and was quickly joined by the others. The game broke up in angry words. Cards went flying as hands greedily reached for the pot of money. Everybody got into the act, including the cheater. Some of the boys got more than their share while others lost out. The losers threatened the winners, especially the cheater. But that was all that happened. No one wanted to end the game. They wanted to continue playing.

Soon another pack of cards appeared on the table. The dealer shuffled the deck, and the game was started again. This time, it was with the promise that there would be no more cheating.

Thomas cites this incident as a lesson about life. No matter the wrongs, people want to keep on playing. All they want is the same opportunity to win as everybody else, rather than be given any special favors. To Thomas the card game was an example of society. It should be left alone without outside interference. In the same way, people should be left alone without government interference—unless they are cheating on the laws.

The best government can do is to apply the same rules of law to everybody, not to the advantage of any particular group. Government should leave people alone to live their own lives.

## Long Live the System

Thomas accepts the way the nation is governed. He believes that there is no need for change. Simply to apply the rules to everyone and in the same way is the only way. This is regardless of sex, race, or religion. Needless to say, the rules must be fair to all.

He started developing these views from his grandfather. An independent-minded man, Myers Anderson had nothing but anger for those who depended on welfare to survive. He was living proof that self-reliance works.

Thomas clearly recalls their last conversation, which was in 1983. The old man explained the difference between principle and popularity. Principle was what a person believed. Popularity was when the majority of

Clarence Thomas is officially welcomed to the Supreme Court by
Chief Justice William Rehnquist.

people agreed. When the principle was unpopular, the choice was difficult. But it is one that each individual has to make. Thomas made his decision, and he was prepared to live with it.

## Cases in Point

As an opponent of school busing, he argues that black children gain nothing from integrated schools. He believes that black children can do quite well in their own schools. He is a critic of the 1954 Supreme Court decision. In *Brown* v. *Board of Education,* the court ruled the segregation of public schools to be illegal. Thomas thinks this decision was based on a false notion: the idea that an all-black school has to be inferior to an integrated school.

He opposes affirmative action. To Thomas, affirmative action means goals and timetables for corporations to hire African Americans. He insists that affirmative action has failed to help them. Most African Americans are still out of the mainstream. What affirmative action means is more money for a few qualified minorities. They are also the ones he sees as members of already well-to-do families who would succeed regardless.

## The Will and the Way

Clarence Thomas has wondered why he has been criticized by African-American leaders. He cannot

United States Supreme Court justices (left to right seated): John P. Stevens, Byron R. White, Chief Justice William H. Rehnquist, Harry A. Blackmun, Sandra Day O'Conner; (standing): David H. Souter, Antonin Scalia, Anthony M. Kennedy, Clarence Thomas.

understand their hostility and is disturbed by it. He has also struck back, publicly mocking these critics. They do nothing but moan and whine, he charges. They complain about the administration at home and apartheid in South Africa. He feels that African-American organizations should work toward improving the education of African Americans. They should try to end such wrongs as poverty and drug abuse.

Thomas has also been through many changes. He is in no way the young man he was at Holy Cross College. During the late 1960s he wore a goatee and a black leather jacket. This image of Clarence Thomas gave way to dark business suits. They were a perfect fit for the conservative man he was to become.

Thomas is also guilty of some of the very things he criticizes. He, too, has worked against apartheid. And he has been critical of the same administration he now defends. While at the EEOC, he gave speeches accusing the Republican Party of ignoring African-American voters.

In one way Clarence Thomas is, indeed, unique. In another way he is representative of most African Americans. Like them, he is of many minds and contradictions. He identifies himself as "black and proud." As a critic and defender of his people, he is also criticized and defended by them.

On his way to the Supreme Court, Thomas helped

Clarence Thomas making the most of a day off and away from his judiciary duties.

destroy a popular racial myth. It is one he did not intend, but for which he may feel proud. He helped show that not all African Americans are alike—uneducated, liberal, and members of the Democratic Party. Some are well educated, conservative, and members of the Republican Party. Many of Thomas's supporters at his confirmation hearings displayed these qualities. They were the proof that there is no one African-American community nor one African-American mind.

As there are real differences within this community, there are many differences within this man. The question is: Which Clarence Thomas will serve the court, and for whose good?

# Chronology

1948—Clarence Thomas is born on June 23, in Pin Point, Georgia.

1950—Thomas' father abandons family.

1955—Thomas' mother relocates the family to Savannah, Georgia.

1956—Clarence and his brother Myers move in with their grandfather, Myers Anderson.

1964—Attends St. John Vianney Minor Seminary.
-1967

1967—Enrolls at Immaculate Conception Seminary; leaves after eight months.

1968—Transfers to Holy Cross College.

1971—Graduates from Holy Cross College with honors; marries Kathy Ambush.

1973—Son, Jamal, is born.

1974—Receives law degree from Yale University.

1974—Serves as assistant attorney general in Missouri
-1977  under Attorney General John Danforth.

1977—Serves as legal counsel for the Monsanto
-1979  Company.

1979—Appointed as Senator John Danforth's legal assistant in Washington, D.C.

1981—Appointed by President Reagan as Assistant Secretary for Civil Rights in the U.S. Department of Education.

1982—Appointed by President Reagan as Chairman of the Equal Employment Opportunity Commission (EEOC).

1984—Thomas and Kathy Ambush divorce.

1987—Marries Virginia Lamp.

1990—Appointed as judge on the Washington, D.C. Court of Appeals.

1991—Controversial nomination by President Bush of Thomas for associate justice of the U.S. Supreme Court; hard-fought confirmation; sworn in on October 18.

1992—Along with nine others, receives the Horatio Alger Award.

# Further Reading

## Books

Alfred, Lisa. *Thurgood Marshall, Supreme Court Justice.* New York: Chelsea House, 1990.

Coulter, E. Merton. *Georgia, A Short History.* Chapel Hill, N.C.: University of North Carolina Press, 1960.

Emmens, Carol A. *An Album of the Sixties.* New York: Franklin Watts, 1981.

King, Spencer B. *Georgia Voices—A Documentary History to 1872.* Athens, Ga.: University of Georgia Press, 1966.

Lawson, Don. *Landmark Supreme Court Cases.* Hillside, N.J.: Enslow Publishers, Inc., 1987.

Stein, Conrad R. *Cornerstones of Freedom—The Story of the Powers of the Supreme Court.* Chicago: Children's Press, 1989.

## Articles

Foote, C. "Doubting Thomas: A Test for Black Conservatism." *Black Enterprise,* October 1991, p.13.

Simson, M. "Clarence Thomas and the Supreme Court." *Publishers Weekly,* December 6, 1991, pp. 37–38.

Tarshia, L. "Changing of the Guard." *Scholastic Update.* (Teachers' edition), November 1, 1991, pp. 6–8.

"Clarence Thomas Rise From Poverty to Supreme Court Nominee." *Jet.* July 22, 1991, pp. 5–10.

"Testing to Uncover Unfair Hiring." *Nation's Business,* February, 1992, pp. 36–37.

"Thomas Asks First Question on Court." *Jet,* November 25, 1991, p. 14.

# Index

## H

Hill, Anita, 74, 76, 81
Holy Cross (College of the),
   44, 46–48, 95

## I

Immaculate Conception
   Seminary, 39, 43

## J

"Jim Crow" laws, 26
Johnson, Andrew, 22

## K

Kennebunkport, Maine, 7
King, Martin Luther Jr., 26, 39

## L

Lamp, Virginia, 61, 77, 78,
   80
Lincoln, Abraham, 20, 22

## M

Maddox, Lester G., 26
Malcolm X, 45
Marshall, Thurgood, 71, 78
Massachusetts, 44, 46
   Worcester, 44–47
Missouri, 55
Monsanto Company, 55
"Mother City of Georgia," 23

## N

National Association for the
   Advancement of
   Colored People
   (NAACP), 23, 26

National Negro Business
   League, 23
New Haven Legal Assistance
   Program, 50
New York City, New York
   61

## O

Oakland, California, 46
O'Conner, Sandra Day, 71
Oglehorpe, James, 20

## P

Philadelphia, Pennsylvania,
   63

## R

Reagan, Ronald, 55
Reconstruction, 22
Rehnquist, William H., 85,
   89, 92
Republican party, 56, 74,
   95, 97

## S

Saint John Vianney Minor
   Seminary, 6, 36, 37,
   43
Savannah State College, 11
Senate Judiciary Committee,
   74
Sherman, Gen. William T.,
   20–22
South Africa, 47
Supreme Court, U.S., 7, 9,
   13, 63–69, 71–73, 76,
   80, 83, 85–87, 93, 95